JKJC

D0876206

FIELD GUIDES
FOR KIDS

INSECTS AND
ARACHNIDS

Carla Mooney

Abdo Reference

An Imprint of Abdo Publishing | abdobooks.com

CONTENTS

Insects and arachnids are some of the most abundant creatures on Earth. They live almost everywhere, from rain forests to deserts, and they come in a vast array of shapes and colors. Among them are some of the oldest creatures on the planet. Scientists estimate that some species date back as far as 400 million years.

WHAT ARE INSECTS LIKE?

Insects are the largest group in the animal kingdom, with about 1.5 million known species. And there may be many more insect species that people have not yet identified. In fact, some scientists estimate that there may be more than ten million insect species on Earth. Insects include flies, beetles, butterflies, moths, ants, wasps, bees, and more. While many insects are tiny, some can grow to be more than 7 inches (18 cm) long.

Insects are highly diverse, but they all have these things in common:

- All insects have hard external coverings called exoskeletons.

- Insect bodies are divided into three regions: the head, thorax, and abdomen.

- On their heads, insects have a pair of antennae that they use to sense smell and taste.

- Insects have three pairs of legs attached to the thorax. Some insects also have wings attached to the thorax.

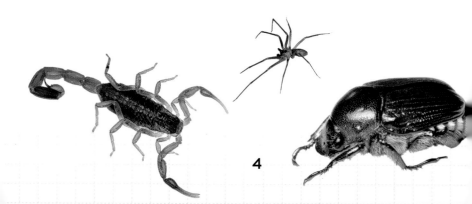

WHAT ARE ARACHNIDS LIKE?

There are more than 60,000 species of arachnids. This group includes spiders, ticks, mites, scorpions, pseudoscorpions, and harvestmen, which are also known as daddy longlegs.

Arachnids have some key features in common:

- Arachnids have eight jointed legs and hard exoskeletons.

- An arachnid's body is made up of two sections: the cephalothorax and the abdomen.

- The cephalothorax is the front part of the body. It contains the head and thorax. An arachnid has four pairs of legs attached to the cephalothorax.

- The rear section of the body is called the abdomen.

- Arachnids have a pair of jointed jaws called chelicerae. Unlike insects, arachnids do not have antennae or wings. To feed, arachnids typically suck blood and fluids from the bodies of other organisms.

WHAT ROLES DO INSECTS AND ARACHNIDS PLAY?

Insects and arachnids crawl, walk, jump, swim, and fly in a variety of habitats around the globe. They are an essential part of the food chain. Some serve as food for larger animals. Others hunt for prey. These creatures also serve as pollinators for many flowering plants. Insects and arachnids are an important part of the world's ecosystems.

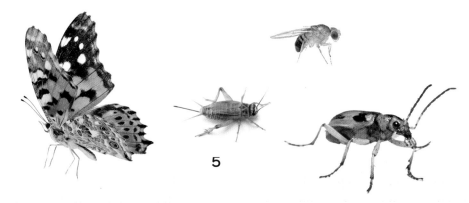

HOW TO USE THIS BOOK

Tab shows the insect
or arachnid category.

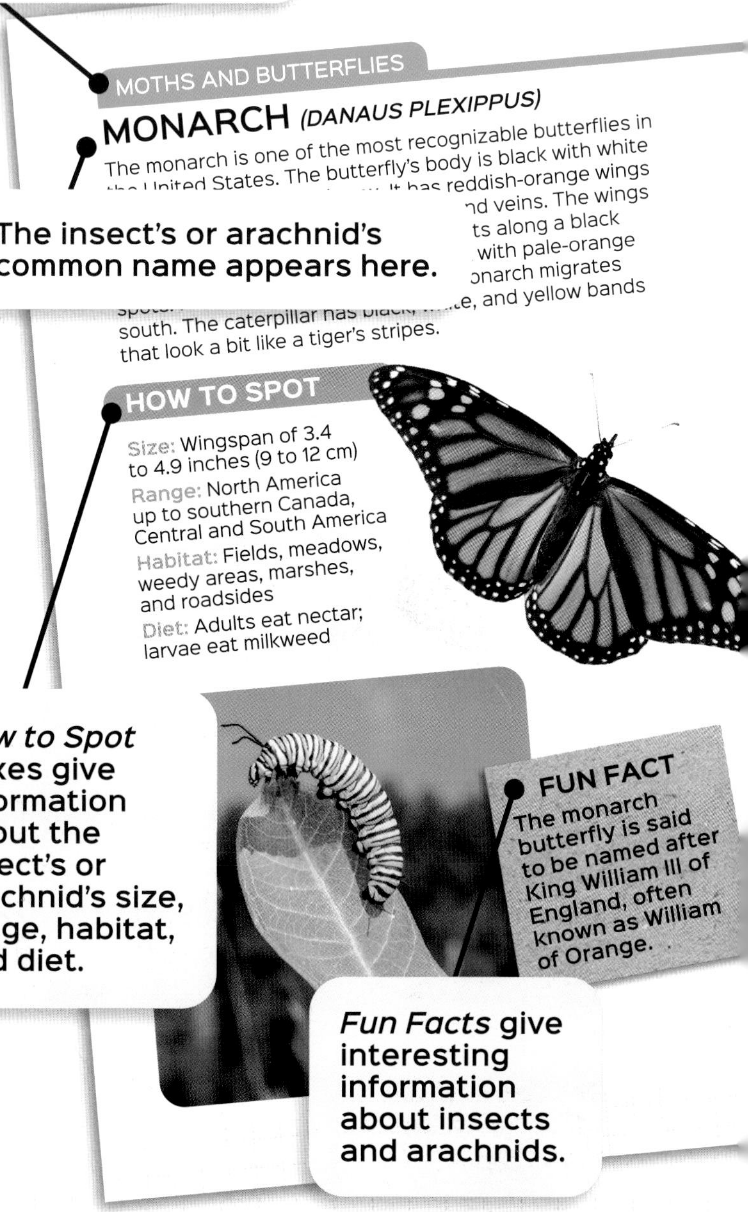

MOTHS AND BUTTERFLIES

MONARCH *(DANAUS PLEXIPPUS)*

The monarch is one of the most recognizable butterflies in
the United States. The butterfly's body is black with white
~~...~~ It has reddish-orange wings
~~...~~ nd veins. The wings

The insect's or arachnid's
common name appears here.

ts along a black
with pale-orange
onarch migrates
spots. The caterpillar has black, white, and yellow bands
that look a bit like a tiger's stripes.

HOW TO SPOT

Size: Wingspan of 3.4
to 4.9 inches (9 to 12 cm)
Range: North America
up to southern Canada,
Central and South America
Habitat: Fields, meadows,
weedy areas, marshes,
and roadsides
Diet: Adults eat nectar;
larvae eat milkweed

How to Spot
boxes give
information
about the
insect's or
arachnid's size,
range, habitat,
and diet.

FUN FACT

The monarch
butterfly is said
to be named after
King William III of
England, often
known as William
of Orange.

Fun Facts give
interesting
information
about insects
and arachnids.

MOURNING CLOAK
(NYMPHALIS ANTIOPA)

The mourning cloak butterfly can be easily identified by its dark brownish-maroon wings with yellow edges and blue spots. The undersides of the wings are a black-brown color with fine lines and lighter brown to yellowish edges. These butterflies are active during the spring and early summer through fall. They hibernate during the winter. The caterpillar is velvety black with red and white spots on its back, and it has several rows of black bristles.

The insect's or arachnid's scientific name appears here.

HOW TO SPOT

Size: Wingspan of 2.9 to 3.4 inches (7 to
Range: North America, Europe, Asia
Habitat: Sunny open areas, gardens, par
woodlands, and along streams and rivers
Diet: Adults eat tree sap and rotting fruits; larvae eat leaves

This paragraph gives information about the insect or arachnid.

Images show the insect or arachnid.

THE MANY USES OF WINGS

Butterflies and moths have two pairs of wings called the forewings and hindwings. The wings serve several roles. Primarily, these insects use their wings to fly. Brightly colored males also use their wings to attract females in courtship displays. Additionally, wings can help butterflies and moths regulate their body temperatures and provide camouflage to avoid predators.

65

Sidebars provide additional information about the topic.

BLUE BOTTLE FLY
(CALLIPHORA VOMITORIA)

Blue bottle flies live near humans or domestic animals. These flies are large and hairy with metallic-blue abdomens. A blue bottle fly has a gray head, black sides, and large red eyes. Adult blue bottle flies are most active during the spring and fall. Females lay their eggs on meat, decaying plant matter, or infected wounds. Females are attracted to meat and often enter open houses. When they can't find an exit, they buzz loudly.

HOW TO SPOT

Size: 0.4 to 0.6 inches (10 to 14 mm) long

Range: Europe, Africa, and the Americas

Habitat: Pastures, barnyards; near decaying meat, rotting vegetation, open wounds, and dung

Diet: Rotting meat, wounds, and liquid from decaying flesh

FUN FACT

The blue bottle fly has an area of reddish coloring on its head that is known as a beard.

BULB FLY *(MERODON EQUESTRIS)*

The bulb fly has a black body with bands of yellow, orange, or tan hairs. With its colored bands, this fly often looks like a small bumblebee. Its legs are black, and its wings are clear. This fly has a wide head that is broader than its thorax. During the spring and summer, bulb flies travel from flower to flower to drink nectar.

HOW TO SPOT

Size: 0.4 to 0.5 inches (10 to 13 mm) long
Range: Most of North America, Europe, and Asia
Habitat: Parks, gardens, meadows, and other places where flowers grow
Diet: Nectar and pollen

CRANE FLY *(TIPULA PALUDOSA)*

The crane fly looks like a giant mosquito. It has six long, thin legs that are very fragile. Often, the fly's legs drop off and regrow. Its abdomen can be gray, brown, or yellow. Sometimes it has a dark mark along its body. The male crane fly has a blunt tip on the end of its abdomen. The female has a pointed tip that she uses to push her eggs into the dirt. The fly has large, translucent wings and large, black antennae with up to 19 segments.

HOW TO SPOT

Size: About 1 inch (25 mm) long
Range: Across the Northern Hemisphere
Habitat: Grasslands, parks, and gardens
Diet: Adults rarely feed but sometimes drink nectar

HALTERES

The crane fly uses its halteres to help it balance during flight. These are small, dumbbell-shaped organs located behind the wings. During flight, the halteres tell the fly how its body is rotating. They send signals to the fly's wing muscles to correct its position in the air.

DRONE FLY *(ERISTALIS TENAX)*

The drone fly looks similar to a honeybee in size and color. It has a dark-brown to black body with yellow-orange markings on its abdomen. Short brownish-yellow hairs cover its thorax and part of its abdomen. The drone fly has two wings. Males have large, close-set eyes, while females have smaller eyes that are more widely spaced.

HOW TO SPOT

Size: About 0.5 to 0.6 inches (13 to 15 mm) long

Range: Every continent except Antarctica

Habitat: Meadows, fields, and near flowers

Diet: Nectar and pollen

FUN FACT
The female drone fly can lay eggs in carcasses.

DUNG FLY *(SCATOPHAGA STERCORARIA)*

The dung fly is often found on the fresh feces of large mammals, including horses, cattle, sheep, and deer. The fly is bright yellow to yellow-brown in color. It is covered with short, upright hairs. Its legs are long and hairy, and it has red eyes. Its wings are yellow-brown near the base and clear near the tips. The dung fly lays its eggs on manure. When the larvae hatch, they tunnel into the dung and feed. The dung fly is predatory. It attacks and eats other flies.

HOW TO SPOT

Size: 0.3 to 0.4 inches (8 to 10 mm) long

Range: Across the Northern Hemisphere

Habitat: Barnyards and pastures near the fresh feces of large mammals

Diet: House flies and other adult insects

12

FRUIT FLY *(DROSOPHILA MELANOGASTER)*

The fruit fly is attracted to the smell of ripe or rotting fruit, which is how it got its name. It has a short body that is yellow-brown in color. Its oval wings extend past its abdomen. The fruit fly has a round head with short antennae and large, bright-red, compound eyes. The fruit fly does not have biting mouthparts. Instead, its mouth sucks up liquids such as nectar and plant juice. The female is slightly bigger than the male. The female's abdomen has a pointed tip while the male's abdomen is rounded.

HOW TO SPOT

Size: 0.1 inches (3 mm) long
Range: Every continent except Antarctica
Habitat: Orchards, fields, forests, and other places near fruit
Diet: Plant juices

FUN FACT
The fruit fly has a very short life cycle. It may be as brief as ten days in warm weather.

13

GIANT ROBBER FLY
(PROCTACANTHUS RODECKI)

The giant robber fly is a large, hairy fly. It has a long, slender body with a tapering abdomen. Its body and legs are covered with stiff bristles that are blackish brown or beige in color. The legs have white hair too. The giant robber fly is a fast and powerful flier and an aggressive hunter. In the air it uses its long legs to capture prey. It attacks wasps, bees, dragonflies, grasshoppers, and other flies. It makes a loud buzzing sound when in flight.

HOW TO SPOT

Size: 1 to 1.1 inches (25 to 28 mm) long
Range: Worldwide
Habitat: Pastures, meadows, and open fields
Diet: Bees and other insects

FUN FACT
The male giant robber fly is territorial. It chases or captures any male that enters its territory.

GREATER BEE FLY
(BOMBYLIUS MAJOR)

The greater bee fly has long hairs on its thorax and abdomen. The hairs are black, brown, and yellow and give the fly the appearance of a fuzzy bee. Its wings are clear with a brown or black pattern along the bottom half. This fly is often active on bright, sunny days. It is commonly spotted sipping nectar from wildflowers using the long, stiff proboscis jutting from its head. It is also seen in sunny woodland areas. As it hovers over flowers, the fly's wings beat rapidly and create a high-pitched whine.

HOW TO SPOT

Size: 0.5 to 0.6 inches (13 to 15 mm) long
Range: North America, Europe, and Asia
Habitat: Woodlands, meadows, open fields, and gardens
Diet: Nectar

GREEN BOTTLE FLY
(LUCILIA SERICATA)

The common green bottle fly is metallic green with black markings. Some have a coppery green color. This fly has black, bristle-like hairs on its back. It also has black antennae and legs. Its wings are mostly clear with light-brown veins. The green bottle fly can often be spotted near garbage, feces, and dead animals. These flies are usually active on bright, sunny days in places where humans and animals live.

HOW TO SPOT

Size: 0.4 inches (10 mm) long

Range: Worldwide, especially in the Northern Hemisphere

Habitat: Dead animals and fish, garbage, feces, and open wounds

Diet: Decomposing animals and plant matter

HOUSE MOSQUITO *(CULEX PIPIENS)*

The house mosquito is a common night-flying mosquito. This mosquito has a light-brown or grayish-brown body and matching brown wings. It has lighter-colored bands on its abdomen. The mosquito's brown-colored mouthpart is long and thin to help it suck up fluids.

HOW TO SPOT

Size: 0.2 to 0.4 inches (5 to 10 mm) long

Range: Found in many regions worldwide and throughout North America

Habitat: Swamps, ponds, and bodies of stagnant water

Diet: Blood from humans and birds, plant juices, and nectar

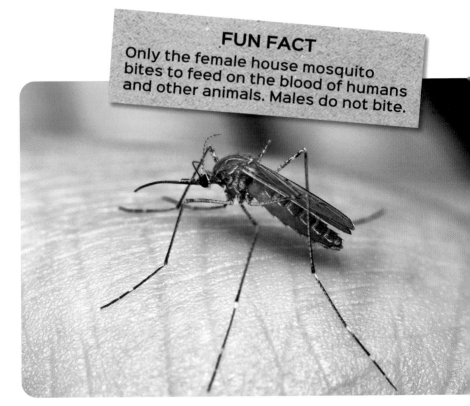

FUN FACT
Only the female house mosquito bites to feed on the blood of humans and other animals. Males do not bite.

HOUSEFLY *(MUSCA DOMESTICA)*

The housefly is a well-known pest often found in homes, on farms, and around garbage dumps. It has a gray thorax with four narrow black stripes running from front to back. Its abdomen is gray or yellowish with dark markings at the midline and on the sides. The fly's clear wings are set at an angle, giving the insect a triangular shape. The housefly produces chemicals from its mouthparts to liquefy its food. Then it sucks up the partially digested food. The housefly is active during the day and rests on ceilings, trees, grasses, and other spots at night.

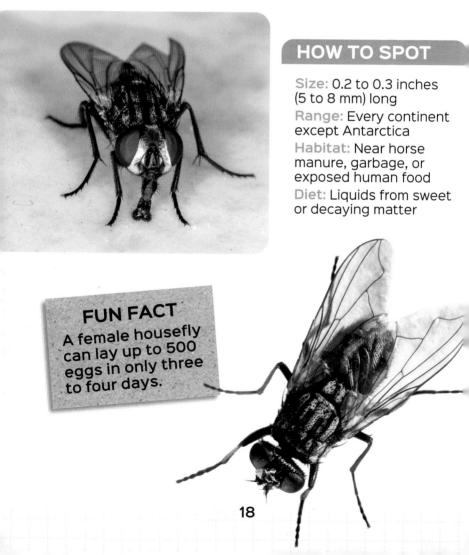

HOW TO SPOT

Size: 0.2 to 0.3 inches (5 to 8 mm) long

Range: Every continent except Antarctica

Habitat: Near horse manure, garbage, or exposed human food

Diet: Liquids from sweet or decaying matter

FUN FACT

A female housefly can lay up to 500 eggs in only three to four days.

THICK-HEADED FLY
(PHYSOCEPHALA TEXANA)

The thick-headed fly has a long, thin body. As its name suggests, the fly's head is thicker than its thorax. Thick-headed flies are reddish brown in color and often have yellow markings. The back of the thick-headed fly's thorax has three black stripes. The abdomen is red with bands of yellow dusting and large, black spots. The two wings are usually clear and sometimes have dark markings. These flies are often found near flowers and use their long mouthparts to sip nectar.

HOW TO SPOT

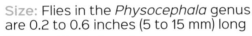

Size: Flies in the *Physocephala* genus are 0.2 to 0.6 inches (5 to 15 mm) long
Range: North America
Habitat: Open areas such as meadows, parks, and brushlands near flowers
Diet: Nectar

ASIAN LONG-HORNED BEETLE
(ANOPLOPHORA GLABRIPENNIS)

The Asian long-horned beetle has a glossy black body. It has approximately 20 white spots on each wing cover. The beetle also has long antennae, about 1.3 to 1.5 times the length of its body. Its antennae are striped with white and black. The beetle's legs are a white-blue color. Female beetles lay eggs in hardwood trees. Larvae bore into the trees and feed on the bark and wood. Adult beetles depart the infested trees. They leave behind round exit holes and piles of sawdust.

HOW TO SPOT

Size: 0.8 to 1.4 inches (20 to 36 mm) long

Range: Temperate zones of East Asia and the United States

Habitat: Hardwood forests and other areas with hardwood such as warehouses

Diet: Leaves, twigs, and plant matter

BIG SAND TIGER BEETLE
(CICINDELA FORMOSA)

The big sand tiger beetle has a distinctive patch of dark-red or purple coloring on its back over a white-ivory background. The shape of this coloring varies by beetle, but it is typically wider at the top and thinner at the bottom. This beetle has six legs and two very long antennae. The big sand tiger beetle is one of the insect world's fiercest predators. It uses the two mandibles located below its antennae to hunt insects and spiders. Because of its large size, this beetle warms up more slowly and becomes active later in the morning than other beetles.

HOW TO SPOT

Size: 0.6 to 0.7 inches (15 to 18 mm) long

Range: North America

Habitat: Dry, sandy areas of blowouts, sand dunes, and sand hills

Diet: Small insects and spiders

FUN FACT
The big sand tiger beetle is better at flying than landing. It often tumbles to the ground when it tries to land.

BOLL WEEVIL *(ANTHONOMUS GRANDIS)*

The adult boll weevil is a small, round-bodied beetle. It has a long snout that extends about half of its body length. Its color is typically grayish black to brown with yellowish hair-like scales. On the inside of its front legs, the boll weevil has a distinct double-toothed spur. In the spring, the boll weevil mates and lays eggs inside a cotton plant. This beetle is active during the summer.

HOW TO SPOT

Size: 0.2 to 0.3 inches (4 to 8 mm) long

Range: Central America, Mexico, Cuba, and the southern United States

Habitat: Areas where cotton is grown

Diet: Cotton seedpods (bolls), cotton flower buds, and related plants

FUN FACT

To protect cotton crops, scientists have inserted a gene into the cotton plant's DNA that causes the plant to produce a compound that is toxic to the boll weevil.

DESTROYING COTTON CROPS

Historically, the boll weevil was a pest for cotton farmers in the southern United States. When weevils infested the cotton bolls, the bolls turned yellow and fell off the plant. This ruined the cotton fibers. Sometimes an infestation caused the entire cotton plant to produce few bolls.

BOMBARDIER BEETLE
(PHEROPSOPHUS AEQUINOCTIALIS)

The bombardier beetle is a species of ground beetle common in Central and South America. The beetle's head and body can be yellow to red in color. Its hardened wing cases usually have two large, black spots that join where the cases meet. The bombardier beetle is nocturnal and spends the day hiding under logs, stones, or grasses. At night it emerges from its hiding spot to run along river beaches and sandy trails.

HOW TO SPOT

Size: 0.6 to 0.8 inches (15 to 20 mm) long
Range: Central and South America
Habitat: Riverbanks, sandbars, and soils near fresh water
Diet: Crickets, insects, plants, and fruits

A DEFENSIVE SPRAY

When in danger, the bombardier beetle can produce a hot, powerful defensive chemical spray. The spray shoots as a fine mist from the tip of the beetle's abdomen, creating a popping sound. The beetle can aim its spray in any direction to deter a potential predator.

DELTA FLOWER SCARAB
(TRIGONOPELTASTES DELTA)

The delta flower scarab is a medium-size beetle. The plate-like structure on its back has a yellow border with a yellow triangle in the middle. The beetle's wing cases are orange-brown with dark spots or markings. Yellowish scales line the beetle's underside. It has antennae with ten segments. It uses its mouthparts to sip pollen or nectar. This beetle is most active during the late spring and summer. It is commonly found near flowers in meadows and grassy areas.

FUN FACT
The word *delta* in the beetle's name comes from the Greek letter delta, which looks like a triangle.

HOW TO SPOT

Size: 0.3 to 0.4 inches (8 to 10 mm) long
Range: Southeastern United States from Florida to eastern Texas
Habitat: Woodlands, meadows, and tall grasses near flowers
Diet: Pollen and nectar

DOGBANE LEAF BEETLE
(CHRYSOCHUS AURATUS)

Dogbane leaf beetles have long, oval shapes. These beetles have a distinct iridescent blue-green color. A dogbane leaf beetle's wing cases are shiny with a coppery color. Its legs and antennae are blue-black in color. Its antennae are long and have 12 joints. The beetle's mandibles are blunt and made for eating plants. It moves from plant to plant within an area of host plants.

HOW TO SPOT

Size: 0.3 to 0.4 inches (8 to 10 mm) long

Range: Southern Canada and most of the United States

Habitat: Near dogbane plants, especially Indian hemp and spreading dogbane

Diet: Dogbane plant leaves and milkweed

25

DRUGSTORE BEETLE
(STEGOBIUM PANICEUM)

The drugstore beetle is a tiny, reddish-brown beetle. It has rows of fine hairs on its wing cases. The wing cases also have parallel rows of deep pits. The beetle's antennae are smooth and end in three segments. The drugstore beetle eats a wide variety of food and materials, including flour, dry mixes, breads, cookies, chocolates, and spices. It also feeds on materials such as wood, hair, leather, horn, and museum specimens. It is a common pest in processed and packaged foods.

HOW TO SPOT

Size: 0.1 inch (3 mm) long
Range: Worldwide; more common in warmer regions
Habitat: Inside stored foods
Diet: A variety of dried herbs and plant material

FUN FACT
The drugstore beetle got its name because it sometimes feeds on prescription drugs.

KITCHEN INVADERS

Drugstore beetles are commonly found in kitchens and pantries. They often live in foods that are kept in open or unsecured containers. They lay their eggs in grain, flour, bread, pasta, cereals, and rice. When they can't find these things, they can survive for weeks without food.

EASTERN EYED CLICK BEETLE
(ALAUS OCULATUS)

Eastern eyed click beetles are thin, long beetles. They are known for the clicking noises they make when moving fast to escape danger. The beetle has a stiff spine on its belly that snaps with force to propel the beetle away from a predator. The snap makes the click sound. When a beetle is stuck on its back, the snap's force can be so powerful that it flips the beetle onto its feet.

HOW TO SPOT

Size: 1 to 1.8 inches (25 to 46 mm) long

Range: United States east of the Rocky Mountains

Habitat: Woodlands, especially near rotting timber

Diet: Adults eat little; larvae eat plant roots

FUN FACT
There are more than 900 species of click beetles living in North America.

GIANT STAG BEETLE
(LUCANUS ELAPHUS)

The giant stag beetle is the largest stag beetle in North America. It has a long, thin body with a flattened back. This beetle is reddish brown and shiny in color. It has black antennae and legs. A male giant stag beetle has a wide head with a crest above the eyes. It also has giant jaws that look like antlers. A female has a narrower head and a smaller jaw. Males use their giant jaws to fight other males for females. At night, the beetles are attracted to light, and they can often be spotted flying at dusk.

HOW TO SPOT

Size: 1.2 to 2.4 inches (30 to 60 mm) long

Range: North America, from North Carolina to the northeastern United States

Habitat: Woodlands and forests

Diet: Sap, plant fluids, and ripe fruit juices

FUN FACT
Female stag beetles release chemicals that attract male beetles.

JAPANESE BEETLE
(POPILLIA JAPONICA)

The Japanese beetle has a bright metallic-green or copper body. Its hardened wing covers are grooved and reddish brown in color. The beetle's underside has grayish hair. On the sides of its abdomen, the beetle has five distinct white tufts of hair. The tip of the beetle's abdomen has two white patches. The beetle feeds during the day, eating nearly 300 species of plants, vegetables, shrubs, and trees.

HOW TO SPOT

Size: 0.4 to 0.5 inches (10 to 12 mm) long

Range: East Asia, southeastern Canada, and the eastern and midwestern United States

Habitat: Open woods, meadows, farms, and gardens

Diet: Foliage and flowers

FUN FACT

A swarm of Japanese beetles can strip a peach tree in only 15 minutes, leaving nothing but bare branches and fruit pits.

PYRALIS FIREFLY *(PHOTINUS PYRALIS)*

The pyralis firefly, also known as the big dipper firefly, is actually a type of beetle. The firefly is dark brown. Its head has a rounded cover with a yellow border and two orange spots. The firefly has two pairs of wings. The first pair of wings is dark brown with a yellow border. This pair forms covers, known as elytra, over the second pair of wings. The firefly has a light-producing organ on its abdomen. When it lights up, it flashes a bright yellow-green color.

FUN FACT

The firefly uses its flashing signals to attract a mate and deter predators.

HOW TO SPOT

Size: 0.4 to 0.6 inches (10 to 15 mm) long
Range: East of the Rocky Mountains
Habitat: Meadows, gardens, parks, and woodland edges
Diet: Insects, earthworms, and snails

RED MILKWEED LEAF BEETLE
(TETRAOPES TETROPHTHALMUS)

The red milkweed leaf beetle has a narrow, elongated body. It is reddish in color and has four black dots on its pronotum. The beetle's wing cases have patterns of black dots and streaks. Its legs are grayish black with traces of red. Its antennae are smooth. Adult red milkweed leaf beetles are generally solitary. Because they can fly, they easily move from place to place. Adults are active in the early summer to autumn.

HOW TO SPOT

Size: 0.3 to 0.6 inches (8 to 15 mm) long
Range: Eastern United States and Canada
Habitat: Near milkweed plants
Diet: Leaves, stems, and flowers of the milkweed plant

SEVEN-SPOTTED LADYBUG
(COCCINELLA SEPTEMPUNCTATA)

The seven-spotted ladybug is a medium-size beetle. Its head and thorax are black with yellow or white markings. Its legs and underside are also black. It has orange-red–colored wing cases with up to nine black spots. The ladybug can fly and is mostly active during the day. Adults are active during the spring and dormant in the summer. During the winter months, adult ladybugs gather in groups of about ten to 15, hibernating together in low-lying grasses or between boulders.

HOW TO SPOT

Size: 0.3 inches (8 mm) long
Range: North America, the Middle East, and India
Habitat: Open fields, grasslands, marshes, gardens, and parks
Diet: Small, sap-sucking insects called aphids

FUN FACT
A female ladybug can eat up to 75 aphids in a single day.

SOUTHERN DUNG BEETLE
(ONTHOPHAGUS AUSTRALIS)

The southern dung beetle is black and shiny. It has a short, broad head with prominent, oval eyes. The beetle has large wings and distinctive segmented antennae. Southern dung beetles are typically active during the late summer and fall. They are known for rolling the feces, or dung, of larger animals into balls. The balls of dung serve as food or as places to lay eggs.

HOW TO SPOT

Size: Dung beetles in the genus *Onthophagus* are 0.1 to 0.4 inches (2 to 11 mm) long
Range: Southeastern Australia
Habitat: Manure in open pastures
Diet: Dung

BALD-FACED HORNET
(DOLICHOVESPULA MACULATA)

The bald-faced hornet is actually a wasp. It got the name "bald-faced" from its white face and black body. This wasp has three white stripes at the end of its body. Bald-faced hornets are a social species. They live in colonies of hundreds to thousands of wasps. The wasps build a ball-shaped paper nest in trees or shrubs. They create the nest by collecting and chewing wood fibers, then forming those fibers into a nest.

HOW TO SPOT

Size: Workers are 0.5 to 0.6 inches (13 to 15 mm) long; queens are 0.7 to 0.8 inches (18 to 20 mm) long

Range: Southern Canada and the United States

Habitat: Forest edges, meadows, parks, and gardens

Diet: Yellow jackets, flies, nectar, and sap

BLACK-AND-GOLD BUMBLEBEE
(BOMBUS AURICOMUS)

The black-and-gold bumblebee is one of the largest bumblebee species. Its body is covered with short hairs of even length. The female workers and the queen have black faces with a few scattered yellow hairs. The male bumblebee has a mostly yellow face and large eyes. The bee's thorax is largely black with some yellow hairs. Its abdomen has yellow and black hairs, and the tip is black. The black-and-gold bumblebee is social and lives in a colony with other bumblebees.

HOW TO SPOT

Size: Workers are 0.3 to 0.5 inches (8 to 13 mm) long; queens are 0.8 to 1 inch (20 to 25 mm) long

Range: Eastern United States and Canada

Habitat: Grasslands, farmlands, and fields

Diet: Nectar and pollen

FUN FACT

The bumblebee carries pollen and nectar totaling about 25 percent of its body weight back to the nest.

THE QUEEN'S ROLE

Each spring, the black-and-gold bumblebee queen emerges from hibernation. She finds a new nest site for the colony and lays eggs. She forages for food and takes care of the colony until the first worker bees emerge. Then the queen stays in the nest to lay more eggs.

BLACK-AND-YELLOW MUD DAUBER *(SCELIPHRON CAEMENTARIUM)*

The black-and-yellow mud dauber is a common black wasp with yellow markings, black antennae, and black eyes. A long, thin, black waist connects its thorax and abdomen. Yellow markings vary by individual wasp. The wasp's abdomen is mostly black, and it has mainly yellow-marked legs. This wasp is not aggressive, and it seldom stings. Adults are active from spring through the fall.

HOW TO SPOT

Size: 1 inch (25 mm) long

Range: The Americas, Asia, Europe, Australia, and some Pacific islands

Habitat: A variety of structures, including rock ledges, bridges, barns, garages, attics, porches, and more

Diet: Nectar

FUN FACT

Black-and-yellow mud daubers collect mud balls at the edges of bodies of water and use them to build rectangular nests.

36

BROWN-WINGED STRIPED SWEAT BEE *(AGAPOSTEMON SPLENDENS)*

The brown-winged striped sweat bee has a distinctive metallic blue-green color and brown wings. It has black antennae and legs. The male bee has black and yellow bands on its abdomen. Like all species of sweat bees, the brown-winged striped sweat bee is attracted to perspiration because of the moisture and salts. This bee builds its nest in the ground or in wood. The bee is an important pollinator of many wildflowers. Females collect pollen to put in the nest for larvae to eat after hatching.

Male

HOW TO SPOT

Size: 0.4 inches (10 mm) long

Range: North Dakota to Maine, south to Texas and Florida

Habitat: Fields, gardens, grasslands, and other open spaces with flowers

Diet: Nectar and pollen

Female

CALIFORNIA CARPENTER BEE
(XYLOCOPA CALIFORNICA)

The California carpenter bee is a large, black bee with some blue-green tint. This bee appears similar to a bumblebee, but its head is larger and it has only short hairs or no hairs on its abdomen. The male bee's face has a yellow-white center. The male has some lighter markings on its pronotum and first abdominal segment. Female bees chew tunnels into dry wood or lumber, where they store food and lay eggs. The California carpenter bee is an important pollinator of many flowers and plants. This bee is active during the spring and summer.

HOW TO SPOT

Size: 0.8 to 1 inch (20 to 25 mm) long
Range: Western United States and Mexico
Habitat: Forests and meadows
Diet: Nectar and pollen

CICADA KILLER WASP
(SPHECIUS SPECIOSUS)

Cicada killer wasps are among the largest wasps in North America. This wasp has a rust-colored head and thorax. Its abdomen has bright-yellow and black bands. The wasp has six legs that can be yellow to red in color. It also has large, dark-amber wings. Female cicada killer wasps have stingers on the ends of their abdomens. They hunt insects called cicadas to feed their larvae.

HOW TO SPOT

Size: 1.2 to 2 inches (30 to 50 mm) long
Range: United States and Europe
Habitat: Forests, grasslands, parks, and gardens
Diet: Nectar and cicadas

FUN FACT
Cicada killer wasps build their nests underground.

THE CICADA KILLER LIFE CYCLE

Female cicada killer wasps use cicadas as hosts for their eggs. The wasp paralyzes and poisons a cicada. Then she brings it back to the nest and deposits her eggs inside it. When the larvae hatch, they feed off the host cicada.

COMMON EASTERN BUMBLEBEE *(BOMBUS IMPATIENS)*

The common eastern bumblebee is one of North America's most common bumblebees. This bumblebee has short pale-yellow hairs on its thorax. Black hairs cover its head, abdomen, and legs. The male bee has a yellow face, and the female's face is black. The common eastern bumblebee is a social bee. It can form large colonies. The older bees gather pollen during the day while younger bees care for the young. While the bees gather pollen and nectar, they pollinate many plants and flowers. Adult bees chew pollen with their saliva to feed growing bee larvae. When the common eastern bumblebee feels threatened, it may sting.

HOW TO SPOT

Size: 0.3 to 0.8 inches (8 to 20 mm) long

Range: Ontario to Florida, west to North Dakota and East Texas

Habitat: Grasslands, forests, marshes, farms, parks, and gardens

Diet: Nectar and pollen

BEE COMMUNICATION

As social insects, common eastern bumblebees communicate with other bees through touch, vision, wing vibrations, and chemicals called pheromones. The bees send messages about where to find food, the safety of the nest, and their daily activities.

EASTERN CARPENTER BEE
(XYLOCOPA VIRGINICA)

The eastern carpenter bee is large and black or metallic blue-black in color. It lives in the eastern regions of North America and in Central America. It has a large, rounded body with yellow hairs. Its abdomen is black, hairless, and shiny. A female bee has a black face, and a male has a white spot on its face. Female bees can sting. Adults are active in the late spring and again in the late summer before hibernating over the winter months. Females bore tunnels into wood, where they store food and lay eggs.

HOW TO SPOT

Size: 0.8 to 0.9 inches (19 to 23 mm) long
Range: Central America and eastern North America
Habitat: Forests, woodlands, gardens, parks, and houses
Diet: Nectar

FUN FACT
Eastern carpenter bees vibrate their strong muscles to shake pollen from flowers, a method called buzz pollination.

EASTERN YELLOWJACKET
(VESPULA MACULIFRONS)

The eastern yellowjacket is a small wasp with distinct black and yellow lines on its head, thorax, and abdomen. Its body is slightly wider than its head. Males, workers, and queens have differing patterns on their abdomens. The female has a stinger at the end of her abdomen that she can use to repeatedly sting animals in defense of her hive. The yellowjacket has strong jaws that let it capture and chew prey. It also has a tongue for sipping nectar and juices from plants. The eastern yellowjacket is usually peaceful. However, it will attack when it feels threatened. The yellowjacket builds its nest underground.

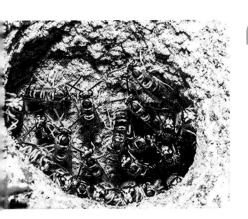

HOW TO SPOT

Size: 0.5 to 0.7 inches (13 to 18 mm) long

Range: Eastern North America

Habitat: Forests, woodlands, gardens, and parks

Diet: Adults eat nectar and juices; larvae eat insects and arthropods

EXECUTIONER WASP
(POLISTES CARNIFEX)

The executioner wasp is known for its extremely painful sting. The wasp is mostly yellow with brown bands on its abdomen. It has large, narrow wings that are reddish brown in color. Its antennae are yellow with a dark base. The wasp's head is yellow, and its crown is black. The executioner wasp is a paper wasp. Paper wasps build their nests by chewing wood fibers until they become paste-like. The wasps use the paste to build nests under the eaves of buildings or hanging from tree branches. When dry, the nests have the consistency of paper.

FUN FACT
Wasps can repeatedly sting their victims because their stingers are smooth. Bees, whose stingers are barbed, can sting only once because the stinger gets stuck in the victim.

HOW TO SPOT

Size: 0.9 to 1.1 inches (23 to 28 mm) long

Range: Parts of the southern United States; Mexico; Central and South America

Habitat: Humid coastal areas such as tropical forests and woodlands

Diet: Adults eat nectar and juices; larvae eat nectar and insects

GOLDEN NORTHERN BUMBLEBEE *(BOMBUS FERVIDUS)*

The golden northern bumblebee is a large, hairy bee. Most of its body is covered in yellow hair, and it has a black stripe of hairs on the thorax between the wings. Its face and head are mostly black, while its wings are dark and smoky colored. Like other bees, golden northern bumblebee workers fly from flower to flower to collect pollen and nectar. They pollinate the flowers along the way. The nectar and pollen are brought back to the nest to feed the queen and bee larvae. These bees have long tongues that allow them to reach into long flowers.

HOW TO SPOT

Size: 0.6 to 0.8 inches (15 to 20 mm) long

Range: North America

Habitat: Open grassy areas, meadows, forest clearings, and open roadsides

Diet: Nectar and honey

FUN FACT

The golden northern bumblebee's hind legs have pollen baskets. These body structures are used to store pollen so the bee can carry it back to the nest.

GREAT GOLDEN DIGGER WASP
(SPHEX ICHNEUMONEUS)

The great golden digger wasp is one of the larger members of the wasp family. It has a bright-orange body, a black-tipped abdomen, and golden hairs. The great golden digger is a solitary wasp and does not live as part of an organized colony. This wasp is most active during the summer. Female wasps tunnel in the open ground, where they lay eggs and store food. Females hunt for insects such as crickets, katydids, and grasshoppers to feed their larvae.

HOW TO SPOT

Size: 0.6 to 0.9 inches (15 to 23 mm) long

Range: The Americas and the Caribbean

Habitat: Meadows with open, sandy areas

Diet: Adults eat nectar and juices; larvae eat crickets, katydids, and grasshoppers

MURDER HORNET *(VESPA MANDARINIA)*

The murder hornet, also known as the Asian giant hornet, is the world's largest hornet. It has a large, yellow head with powerful jaws that it uses to overpower prey. The hornet's thorax is black, while its abdomen has alternating bands of yellow and black. Its body is covered in hair. The hornet also has two pairs of wings. A female murder hornet has a smooth stinger that is nearly 0.4 inches (10 mm) long. Murder hornets are social hornets and live in colonies.

HOW TO SPOT

Size: 1.5 to 2 inches (38 to 51 mm) long
Range: Asia; some colonies spotted in North America in 2019
Habitat: Dense woodlands
Diet: Bees, honeybees, insects, and wasps

FUN FACT
One murder hornet can kill up to 40 honeybees in a single minute.

ATTACKING HONEYBEES

A murder hornet kills a honeybee by detaching the bee's head from its body. Then the hornet chews the bee into a gummy paste that it takes back to the nest for its larvae. Sometimes a group of ten to 20 murder hornets will stage a coordinated attack on an entire honeybee colony.

WESTERN HONEYBEE
(APIS MELLIFERA)

The western honeybee is mostly reddish brown and black in color, with orange and yellow rings on its abdomen. Its head, antennae, and legs are black. Short, pale hairs cover its thorax and lightly cover its abdomen. The honeybee's wings are translucent. The bee has a pollen basket on its hind legs. The western honeybee is a social bee that lives in colonies of up to 80,000 workers and a single queen bee. Colonies build hives in hollow trees and similar spaces.

HOW TO SPOT

Size: 0.4 to 0.8 inches (10 to 20 mm) long

Range: Worldwide

Habitat: Meadows, open wooded areas, and gardens near flowering plants

Diet: Nectar and honey

FUN FACT
Honeybees build their hives out of wax secretions from their bodies. The honeybee queens lay eggs in cells in the wax.

ONE CHANCE TO STING

A honeybee worker has a barbed stinger. The bee can sting only once. When the bee stings its victim, the bee's stinger sticks in the target. The stinger rips out of the bee's abdomen, causing the bee to die.

AFRICAN WEAVER ANT
(OECOPHYLLA LONGINODA)

The African weaver ant is a large ant that varies from orange to dark brown in color. The thorax is covered with fine hairs, while short hairs cover the abdomen. The ant's feet have suction pads that allow it to firmly cling to surfaces. Its antennae have 12 segments. The African weaver has large mandibles with long, triangular teeth. It uses silk produced by its larvae to stitch leaves together and build nests in trees. African weaver ants are aggressive and will attack other ants and insects.

FUN FACT

If their nest is disturbed, thousands of African weaver ants will drop down to attack, bite, and secrete a mild acid on the intruder.

HOW TO SPOT

Size: 0.2 inches (5 mm) long
Range: Sub-Saharan Africa
Habitat: Tropical rain forests
Diet: Insects and ants

ARGENTINE ANT *(LINEPITHEMA HUMILE)*

The Argentine ant is small and brown in color with a flattened head. It has a thin petiole, a structure that connects its thorax and abdomen. The ant's mandibles, antennae, and legs can be yellow, red, or brown. This ant is active year-round and often found near human homes. It lives in large colonies that sometimes join together to form super colonies. Argentine ants are aggressive predators. They will attack other ants and insects to defend their colonies.

HOW TO SPOT

Size: 0.08 to 0.1 inch (2 to 3 mm) long

Range: All continents except Antarctica

Habitat: Forests; fields; and near rivers, homes, buildings, and other areas where humans live

Diet: Insects; nectar; honeydew, liquid secreted by aphids and other insects; and human food

BLACK CARPENTER ANT
(CAMPONOTUS PENNSYLVANICUS)

One part of the black carpenter ant's name comes from its black color. The other part comes from the fact that it creates its nests in damaged wood. It has one petiole connecting its thorax and abdomen. The ant's abdomen has long, pale-yellow or grayish hairs. Carpenter ants are active during the spring and summer. In hot weather, they search for food at night. This ant species does not sting, but individuals will bite and spray a type of acid at predators.

HOW TO SPOT

Size: Workers are 0.2 to 0.6 inches (5 to 16 mm) long; queens average 0.75 inches (19 mm) long

Range: Eastern United States and Canada

Habitat: Logs, tree trunks, timber, and buildings

Diet: Insects, honeydew, fruit juices, sugar grains, and other sweets

FIRE ANT *(SOLENOPSIS GEMINATA)*

The fire ant ranges in color from dull yellow to red or black. It has a large head and jaws. It has two segments between its thorax and abdomen. Fine hair covers its head and abdomen. Its antennae have ten segments, with two at the end forming a structure called a club. Fire ants live in large colonies that may contain hundreds of thousands of worker ants. This species builds nests in the soil that often take the form of large soil mounds. Workers have powerful stings and bites that produce a burning sensation like fire.

HOW TO SPOT

Size: 0.06 to 0.3 inches (2 to 8 mm) long

Range: Most of the United States and southern Canada

Habitat: Fields, woodlands, and open areas in dry to moist soil

Diet: Insects, seeds, poultry, fruits, honeydew, vegetables, and flowers

FUN FACT

Worker fire ants dig underground tunnels that can stretch up to 25 feet (8 m) away from the nest's large soil mound.

51

ODOROUS HOUSE ANT
(TAPINOMA SESSILE)

Odorous house ants are one of the most widespread ant species across North America. This small ant ranges in color from brown to black, with lighter jaws and legs. Worker ants have oval-shaped heads, short thoraxes, and slightly arched bodies. They may have a few light-yellow hairs on their bodies. These ants do not sting, but they can bite. When crushed, odorous house ants emit an unpleasant smell similar to that of rotten coconuts. These ants often build nests in mulch, debris piles, and buildings. Once the ants establish a colony, they are difficult to move.

FUN FACT

Once an odorous house ant finds food, it leaves an invisible scent trail back to its nest so the other worker ants can find the food too.

HOW TO SPOT

Size: 0.09 to 0.17 inches (2 to 4 mm) long

Range: Southern Canada to northern Mexico

Habitat: Forests, meadows, grasslands, parks, gardens, mulch, and dirt piles

Diet: Honeydew, nectar, small insects and spiders, and human food

PHARAOH ANT
(MONOMORIUM PHARAONIC)

The pharaoh ant is a very small ant that is a common indoor pest. The ant's body is yellow to light brown to red and almost transparent. It is smooth and shiny with a tiny waist featuring two knobs that connect its thorax and abdomen. The ant's antennae have 12 segments with a three-segment club at the tip. Pharaoh ants use their antennae to sense vibrations and help them navigate dark areas. These ants often establish colonies in hard-to-reach places in buildings. They do not sting, but they are among the most difficult ants to remove from a home.

HOW TO SPOT

Size: 0.04 to 0.08 inches (1 to 2 mm) long
Range: Worldwide
Habitat: Heated structures and soil in subtropical regions
Diet: Insects and household foods

53

ROUGH HARVESTER ANT
(POGONOMYRMEX RUGOSUS)

The rough harvester ant is reddish brown in color. It has a two-segment waist between its thorax and abdomen. The ant's head has strong mouthparts for chewing seeds and grains. The ant also has hairs on the underside of its head that it uses to carry objects. A female rough harvester ant has a stinger at the tip of the abdomen. During the day, these ants spread out from the colony to gather plants and seeds for the nest. When threatened, harvester ants can sting or bite. When the colony is attacked, these ants will swarm to defend it.

HOW TO SPOT

Size: 0.3 to 0.5 inches (8 to 13 mm) long

Range: Southwestern United States into Mexico

Habitat: Lowlands, bare areas, and sandy areas near roads

Diet: Seeds, grains, and plant materials

WINTER ANT *(PRENOLEPIS IMPARIS)*

The winter ant is common across the United States. Worker winter ants are light to dark brown in color. Queen ants are reddish brown, and males are black. The ant's head is sometimes darker than its midsection and legs. Overall, the ant's body is smooth, shiny, and shaped like an hourglass. It has a one-segment waist between its thorax and abdomen. The winter ant is most active during cool weather, when other ant species are less likely to gather food. During warmer months, these ants close off their nest entrance and become dormant.

HOW TO SPOT

Size: 0.1 to 0.3 inches (3 to 8 mm) long
Range: North America
Habitat: Wooded areas and damp soil with clay
Diet: Dead insects, earthworms, small arthropods, seeds, nectar, honeydew, and decaying fruits

STORING FOOD

Some winter ants act as food storage units for the colony. These ants fill their bellies with nectar. Too big and bloated to move, they hang from the roof of the nest. When food is scarce, the ants will regurgitate the food in their bellies to feed the members of their colony.

BANDED WOOLLYBEAR MOTH
(PYRRHARCTIA ISABELLA)

The banded woollybear moth is a type of tiger moth. It has yellowish-brown forewings with rows of small, black spots. The moth's hindwings are paler than its forewings, are tinted pinkish orange, and have black or gray spots. Adult moths are active from the late winter through the late fall. They are nocturnal and are attracted to lights. The woollybear's caterpillar form is covered in a band of red-orange hair in the middle and a band of black hair on each end.

HOW TO SPOT

Size: Wingspan of 1.6 to 2.1 inches (4 to 5 cm)

Range: Southern Canada, the United States, and northern Mexico

Habitat: Fields, meadows, pastures, and roadsides

Diet: Adults eat nectar; larvae eat plants and trees

FUN FACT
Wet weather lengthens the black bands on the woollybear caterpillar. The red band lengthens as the caterpillar matures.

CABBAGE WHITE *(PIERIS RAPAE)*

The cabbage white is a small- to medium-size butterfly. This butterfly is known for its white wings. The forewings have black tips and black spots, with one spot on males and two spots on females. The butterfly's hindwings can be white, pale yellow, or gray-white. Adult butterflies are active from early spring through late fall. They fly mostly during the day and rest at night. The caterpillar form is a bright-green color and is covered with short hairs. It has yellow stripes on its sides and back.

HOW TO SPOT

Size: Wingspan of 1.8 to 2.3 inches (5 to 6 cm)

Range: Worldwide

Habitat: Open spaces including gardens, grasses, roadsides, and parks in urban and suburban areas

Diet: Adults eat nectar; larvae eat cabbages and other plants in the mustard family

Forewing

Hindwing

CASEMAKING CLOTHES MOTH
(TINEA PELLIONELLA)

The casemaking clothes moth is a small moth. It has long, narrow forewings that are brownish gray in color and fringed with small hairs. The forewings also have one or more dark spots. The moth's hindwings are a pale brown-gray. These moths are active year-round in homes. They prefer dark areas such as closets, basements, and attics. Adult casemaking clothes moths do not feed. However, their larvae eat fabric and can destroy clothing. The casemaking clothes moth encloses itself in an open-ended, silken, tube-shaped case. It makes the case from fibers of materials the larva has eaten. The larva drags the case wherever it goes.

HOW TO SPOT

Size: Wingspan of 0.4 to 0.6 inches (1 to 1.5 cm)

Range: Worldwide

Habitat: Birds' nests and indoors in buildings and structures

Diet: Adults do not feed; larvae eat wool, fur, feathers, and hair

58

CECROPIA MOTH
(HYALOPHORA CECROPIA)

The cecropia moth is the largest moth in North America. Its wingspan can reach up to 6 inches (15 cm). The wings are brownish with white, red, and tan bands. Each wing has a large crescent shape outlined in black. The forewings also have a crescent in an eyespot near the tip. The moth's body is hairy with red and white bands on its abdomen. Adult cecropia moths are active at night during the spring and summer and are attracted to lights. The cecropia caterpillar is pale green with orange, yellow, and blue knobs.

HOW TO SPOT

Size: Wingspan of 4.3 to 6 inches (11 to 15 cm)

Range: Southern Canada and much of the United States

Habitat: Open areas with trees

Diet: Adults do not feed; larvae eat leaves

FUN FACT
Moths have hairy bodies to help them maintain their internal body temperatures.

EYESPOTS

Some butterflies and moths have eyespots. An eyespot is a marking on the wing or tail of a butterfly or moth that looks like an eye. Eyespots may deter predators or trick them into attacking parts of the insect's body that aren't needed for survival.

COMMON WOOD-NYMPH
(CERCYONIS PEGALA)

The common wood-nymph is a familiar butterfly in North America. Common wood-nymphs are brown and have two ringed eyespots on each forewing. Some may have additional smaller eyespots on the hindwings. Butterflies that live in southern and coastal regions are larger and have yellowish patches on the outer forewings. Butterflies that live more inland are smaller and may not have yellow patches. The caterpillar is bright green with two yellow stripes on each side. It has fine, fuzzy hair and two short red tails.

HOW TO SPOT

Size: Wingspan of 1.8 to 3 inches (5 to 8 cm)

Range: Southern Canada and most of the continental United States, except the Southwest and Florida

Habitat: Large, sunny, grassy areas including prairies, open meadows, bogs, and fields

Diet: Adults eat rotting fruits and nectar; larvae eat grasses

GIANT SWALLOWTAIL
(PAPILIO CRESPHONTES)

The giant swallowtail is the largest butterfly in North America. It is a dark-brown to black butterfly with a striking diagonal band of yellow spots across its forewings. The undersides of the wings are mostly yellow. This butterfly is active year-round, though only rarely during midwinter. The caterpillar is brown or olive with buff spots and can sometimes look like a bird dropping.

HOW TO SPOT

Size: Wingspan of 4 to 6.3 inches (10 to 16 cm)
Range: The Americas
Habitat: Woodlands, gardens, and citrus groves
Diet: Adults eat nectar; larvae eat leaves and young plant shoots

FUN FACT
When threatened, the giant swallowtail caterpillar sticks out an orange gland and gives off a bad smell to deter predators.

GRAY HAIRSTREAK
(STRYMON MELINUS)

The gray hairstreak is a small butterfly with gray-purple wings. The undersides of its wings are gray with a white line along the edges. On its hindwings, the butterfly has a black dot within an orange spot. An orange spot can also be found on its head, between the eyes. The gray hairstreak also has a tail on each of its hindwings.

FUN FACT

When a predator approaches, the grey hairstreak can wriggle the tails on its hindwings. The moving tails look like antennae and may trick the predator into attacking the wrong end of the insect.

HOW TO SPOT

Size: Wingspan of 0.9 to 1.4 inches (2 to 4 cm)

Range: Southern Canada to northwestern South America

Habitat: Tropical forests, open woodland areas, meadows, fields, open roadsides, parks, and yards

Diet: Adults eat nectar; larvae eat flowers, fruits, and leaves

LUNA MOTH *(ACTIAS LUNA)*

Luna moths are large, pale-green moths. Each wing has a transparent eyespot. The hindwings have long, curving tails. In the summer, the moth's forewings have a pink, yellow, or reddish-brown color along the leading edge. These beautiful moths are active at night and are drawn to lights. The caterpillar form is bright green and covered with small spots that are black and pink. Yellow lines fall between the caterpillar's segments.

HOW TO SPOT

Size: Wingspan of 3 to 4 inches (8 to 10 cm)

Range: Southern Canada, the United States, and Mexico

Habitat: Hardwood forests

Diet: Adults do not feed; larvae eat leaves of hardwood trees

MONARCH *(DANAUS PLEXIPPUS)*

The monarch is one of the most recognizable butterflies in the United States. The butterfly's body is black with white spots on its head and thorax. It has reddish-orange wings with a pattern of wide black borders and veins. The wings have small white and pale-orange spots along a black border. The tips of the wings are black with pale-orange spots. From August to October, the monarch migrates south. The caterpillar has black, white, and yellow bands that look a bit like a tiger's stripes.

HOW TO SPOT

Size: Wingspan of 3.4 to 4.9 inches (9 to 12 cm)

Range: North America up to southern Canada, Central and South America

Habitat: Fields, meadows, weedy areas, marshes, and roadsides

Diet: Adults eat nectar; larvae eat milkweed

FUN FACT

The monarch butterfly is said to be named after King William III of England, often known as William of Orange.

MOURNING CLOAK
(NYMPHALIS ANTIOPA)

The mourning cloak butterfly can be easily identified by its dark brownish-maroon wings with yellow edges and blue spots. The undersides of the wings are a black-brown color with fine lines and lighter brown to yellowish edges. These butterflies are active during the spring and early summer through fall. They hibernate during the winter. The caterpillar is velvety black with red and white spots on its back, and it has several rows of black bristles.

HOW TO SPOT

Size: Wingspan of 2.9 to 3.4 inches (7 to 8 cm)
Range: North America, Europe, and Asia
Habitat: Sunny open areas, gardens, parks, open woodlands, and along streams and rivers
Diet: Adults eat tree sap and rotting fruits; larvae eat leaves

THE MANY USES OF WINGS

Butterflies and moths have two pairs of wings called the forewings and hindwings. The wings serve several roles. Primarily, these insects use their wings to fly. Brightly colored males also use their wings to attract females in courtship displays. Additionally, wings can help butterflies and moths regulate their body temperatures and provide camouflage to avoid predators.

PAINTED LADY *(VANESSA CARDUI)*

The painted lady butterfly has orange-brown wings. Its forewings have black, rounded tips with white spots. Its hindwings have a row of black spots along the edges. The wing's underside has a black, brown, and gray pattern with small eyespots. Painted lady butterflies are active from spring through fall. While they prefer open areas such as fields and meadows, they are very adaptable and can live in a variety of habitats. The caterpillar is grayish brown with black marbling, a yellow stripe on its back, and gray spines.

FUN FACT

The painted lady butterfly makes an annual mass migration that can be up to 9,300 miles (15,000 km) long.

HOW TO SPOT

Size: Wingspan of 2 to 2.9 inches (5 to 7 cm)
Range: Worldwide, except Australia and Antarctica
Habitat: Areas with wide-open areas of vegetation such as fields and meadows
Diet: Adults eat nectar; larvae eat leaves

SPRING AZURE *(CELASTRINA LADON)*

The spring azure butterfly is widespread across most of North America. The butterfly's wings are pale to bright blue in color. The wing's edges have a checkered border on males and a wider black-gray border on females. The undersides of the wings are gray with several darker spots. Adults are active during spring and summer in northern and western regions. In southern regions, these butterflies are active year-round.

HOW TO SPOT

Size: Wingspan of 0.8 to 1.2 inches (2 to 3 cm)

Range: Most of North America

Habitat: Gardens, woodlands, desert foothills, tundra, and other habitats

Diet: Adults eat nectar; larvae eat flowers and fruits

BEDBUG *(CIMEX LECTULARIUS)*

The bedbug is a parasite that feeds on the blood of humans and other animals. The insect is flat, round, and covered in short, stiff hairs. It has small leathery wings that are wider than they are long. Its pronotum is notched and fringed with hairs. The bedbug is active at night. It crawls to find a human host for a blood meal. Before feeding, the bedbug is usually brown in color. After feeding, its body swells and becomes redder.

FUN FACT

The lump or swelling experienced after a bedbug bite is caused by an allergic reaction to the bedbug's saliva.

HOW TO SPOT

Size: 0.2 to 0.3 inches (4 to 7 mm) long
Range: Worldwide
Habitat: Human dwellings in beds, bedding, clothing, carpets, and furniture
Diet: Human blood

GIANT WATER BUG
(LETHOCERUS AMERICANUS)

The giant water bug is brown and flat with an oval shape. It sometimes looks like a dead leaf. It has flattened hind legs that it uses as oars when swimming. It is a fierce predator. When hunting, the bug uses a hook-shaped claw on its forelegs to grab and hold prey. Then the water bug pierces its prey with its sharp beak. It injects a powerful toxin that paralyzes the prey. Then it liquefies the internal parts of the prey's body. The bug sucks up the resulting liquid.

FUN FACT
Water bugs are also called toe biters because they have painful bites.

HOW TO SPOT

Size: 1.6 to 2.5 inches (41 to 64 mm) long
Range: Worldwide
Habitat: Freshwater ponds, marshes, and slow-moving streams
Diet: Insects, tadpoles, and small fish

ﾟEATHING UNDERWATER

giant water bug has a unique adaptation for living in ﾟr. It has breathing tubes at the end of its abdomen. ﾟe tubes reach the water's surface like snorkels. The ﾟr bug can draw in air through the tubes. The air ﾟrs the body through holes in the abdomen.

GREEN PEACH APHID
(MYZUS PERSICAE)

The green peach aphid is a small bug that may be winged or wingless. Winged green peach aphids have black heads and thoraxes and yellow-green abdomens with a large dark patch. Wingless aphids are yellow to green in color. Some have green stripes down the middle or sides of their bodies. The aphid also has cornicles, or tubes, that project from the abdomen. The tubes secrete a defensive fluid. The green peach aphid is considered a pest because of its ability to spread plant viruses.

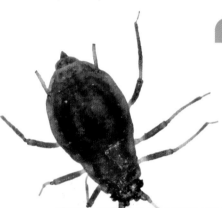

HOW TO SPOT

Size: 0.08 inches (2 mm) long
Range: Worldwide
Habitat: A variety of host plants
Diet: Host plants including lettuce, peach, potato, spinach, tomato, and other vegetables and ornamental crops

LARGE MILKWEED BUG
(ONCOPELTUS FASCIATUS)

The large milkweed bug is bright orangish red and black in color. On the thorax, a black diamond shape is surrounded by an orange border. A thick, black band crosses the middle of the bug's body. The lower ends of its wings are also black. Adult milkweed bugs are active from spring to fall and are typically found in large groups. They can fly from plant to plant to gather food. The bug uses its long mouthpart to pierce and suck food.

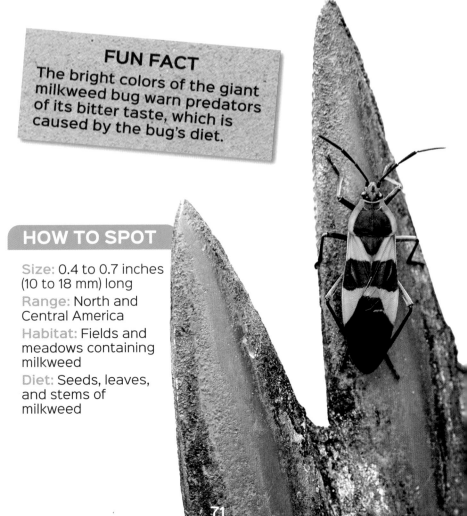

FUN FACT
The bright colors of the giant milkweed bug warn predators of its bitter taste, which is caused by the bug's diet.

HOW TO SPOT

Size: 0.4 to 0.7 inches (10 to 18 mm) long

Range: North and Central America

Habitat: Fields and meadows containing milkweed

Diet: Seeds, leaves, and stems of milkweed

PALE GREEN ASSASSIN BUG
(ZELUS LURIDUS)

The pale green assassin bug has a slender, green body with a narrow head and wings that range from tan to brown. The male is smaller and darker than the female of this species. The bug's head is dark brown or black with red eyes. It has a shield-like shoulder plate with a pair of spines. As its name suggests, the assassin bug preys on other insects. It captures small, soft-bodied prey using a sticky secretion on its forelegs.

FUN FACT

Sometimes the assassin bug waits on a leaf to attack an unsuspecting insect. Other times, it actively hunts its prey.

HOW TO SPOT

Size: 0.5 to 0.8 inches (13 to 20 mm) long

Range: Southeastern Canada, the United States, and Mexico

Habitat: Wooded habitats and along roadsides

Diet: Other insects

RED-BANDED LEAFHOPPER
(GRAPHOCEPHALA COCCINEA)

The red-banded leafhopper is a brightly colored, slender bug native to North and Central America. It has yellow legs and a yellow head with a black stripe through the eyes. Its thorax and wings are striped with bright blue-green and red-orange. As its name suggests, the leafhopper moves by hopping or leaping. It is often found near blackberry and raspberry bushes and ornamental plants such as roses and rhododendrons. When threatened, the leafhopper springs away from potential predators. These bugs are active from the spring through fall.

HOW TO SPOT

Size: 0.3 to 0.4 inches (8 to 10 mm) long

Range: Northern and eastern North America and Central America

Habitat: Meadows and woodlands

Diet: Sap of vines, plants, and shrubs

SQUASH BUG *(ANASA TRISTIS)*

The squash bug is a common pest found on pumpkins and squash. The adult squash bug has an oval body that ranges from gray to black in color. It has orange and brown stripes along the edges of its abdomen. Its wings fold flat over the body. The squash bug uses its mouthparts to suck sap from plants. When it feeds, the squash bug damages the plant and injects a toxic substance that causes the plant to wilt and blacken.

HOW TO SPOT

Size: 0.5 to 1 inch (13 to 25 mm) long

Range: North and Central America

Habitat: Agricultural fields and gardens

Diet: Sap from the stems, leaves, and fruits of melon and squash plants

STINK BUG *(BANASA DIMIATA)*

The stink bug is widespread in North America. This bug gets its name from the unpleasant odor it emits when threatened. It produces a smelly chemical in a gland on its abdomen as a way to deter predators. Although its color can vary, the stink bug typically has a two-color pronotum that is green near the head and dark green or reddish brown toward the abdomen. The stink bug has two pairs of wings. The forewings are longer and cover the hindwings. Stink bugs are active from spring to fall in many types of trees and shrubs.

FUN FACT

The stink bug's smelly chemical attracts other stink bugs. In the fall, the bugs release the chemical when they find a warm place to gather.

HOW TO SPOT

Size: 0.3 to 0.4 inches (8 to 10 mm) long
Range: Southern Canada to northern Mexico
Habitat: Orchards, gardens, and farms
Diet: A variety of trees and shrubs

FAMILIAR BLUET DAMSELFLY
(ENALLAGMA CIVILE)

The familiar bluet damselfly's bright-blue color makes it easy to see as it flies from plant to plant in search of insects to eat. The male has blue around the eyes and black stripes down the thorax. It has a long, thin abdomen that is mostly blue with black spots. The female familiar bluet has a similar shape and markings but has pale-blue or light-brown coloring. The familiar bluet is active in the late spring through fall in most areas. It lives near water and lays its eggs just under the water's surface.

HOW TO SPOT

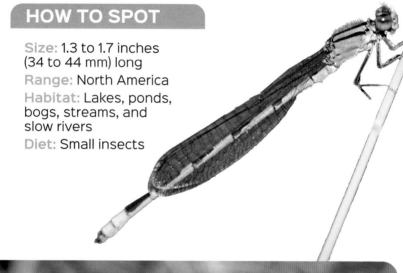

Size: 1.3 to 1.7 inches (34 to 44 mm) long

Range: North America

Habitat: Lakes, ponds, bogs, streams, and slow rivers

Diet: Small insects

FIELD CRICKET
(GRYLLUS PENNSYLVANICUS)

Adult field crickets are black and brown with long antennae. They use their large hind legs to jump powerfully and rapidly. All field crickets make the recognized chirping sound. A cricket's chirping sound occurs when it rubs scrapers on its left forewing across a row of teeth-like structures on its right forewing. The male field cricket creates a three-note song. The female answers with a two-note song. Field crickets are active during the summer and fall. They typically live in small burrows in grassy areas and on the ground underneath plant matter.

HOW TO SPOT

Size: 0.6 to 1 inch (15 to 25 mm) long
Range: North America
Habitat: Grassy areas
Diet: Plants, small fruits, seeds, and insects

FUN FACT

The field cricket chirps more rapidly in warmer weather. Taking the number of chirps in 13 seconds and adding 40 gives an approximate temperature in degrees Fahrenheit.

GREEN DARNER DRAGONFLY
(ANAX JUNIUS)

The green darner dragonfly got its name because it looks like a darning needle. It has large eyes and a short, thick, green thorax with four wings. Its abdomen is long and thin with a black stripe on the back. Males are mostly green with some blue segments on their abdomens. Females can be green, brown, and grayish green in color. Adults are active during the day, dawn, and dusk. They often rest in foliage around ponds and other water sources. As strong fliers, they are successful at hunting prey in the air.

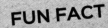

FUN FACT
The green darner dragonfly's four wings move independently. This allows the dragonfly to fly forward and backward and rapidly change directions.

HOW TO SPOT

Size: 2.7 to 3.1 inches (68 to 79 mm) long

Range: North and Central America, the Caribbean, and parts of Asia

Habitat: Areas near rivers, streams, ponds, and other water sources

Diet: Insects

ORIENTAL COCKROACH
(BLATTA ORIENTALIS)

The oriental cockroach, also called a water bug, lives in every country in the world. It is shiny black or dark brown in color. The male has wings that cover approximately 75 percent of its body, while the female has short wing pads. Neither the male nor the female can fly. The oriental cockroach is active year-round. It lives in a variety of places, including basements, cellars, crawl spaces, hollow trees, and stumps. Sometimes a large infestation of oriental cockroaches can be detected by a strong, musty odor.

HOW TO SPOT

Size: 0.7 to 1.2 inches (18 to 30 mm) long
Range: Worldwide
Habitat: Areas containing natural debris and warm, damp, shady areas near the ground
Diet: Garbage, sewage, and decaying organic matter

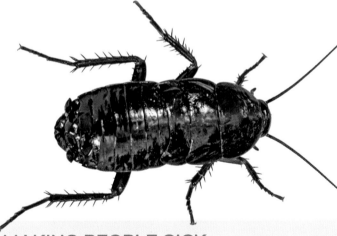

MAKING PEOPLE SICK

As the oriental cockroach crawls through unsanitary areas, it spreads dirt, bacteria, and other germs wherever it walks. By shedding skin and excreting waste products, these cockroaches can contaminate food and spread allergens that trigger allergic reactions and other illnesses in nearby humans.

PRAYING MANTIS *(MANTIS RELIGIOSA)*

The praying mantis gets its name from the way its long front legs sometimes appear to be folded in prayer. The praying mantis has a large, elongated, green or tan body. It has two pairs of wings that stretch past its abdomen. The mantis also has a mobile, triangle-shaped head with large eyes. Adults are active during the late summer and fall. They hunt a variety of insects by day. The praying mantis is a solitary insect. It interacts with another mantis only to mate in late summer.

FUN FACT
The praying mantis can swivel its head 180 degrees to look at its surroundings.

HOW TO SPOT

Size: 2 to 2.6 inches (51 to 66 mm) long
Range: Southern Europe, Asia, Africa, Australia, and North America
Habitat: Meadows
Diet: Caterpillars, butterflies, flies, and some species of moth

SPUR-THROATED GRASSHOPPER

(MELANOPLUS PONDEROSUS)

The spur-throated grasshopper is one of the most common grasshoppers in North America. The grasshopper is typically yellow, green, or pale brown in color. Its body may have bands, spots, or blotches of color on it. It has a blunt projection between the bases of its forelegs that looks like a spur. Its hind legs are often orange or reddish with yellow and brown markings. The spur-throated grasshopper's chewing mouthparts tear away plant tissue. It is known for causing damage to corn, small grains, and other crops.

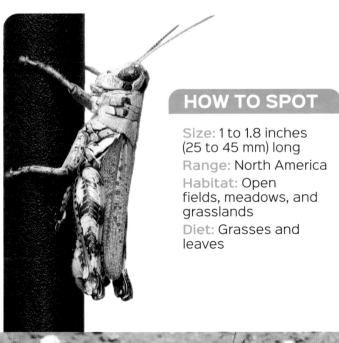

HOW TO SPOT

Size: 1 to 1.8 inches (25 to 45 mm) long

Range: North America

Habitat: Open fields, meadows, and grasslands

Diet: Grasses and leaves

BANDED GARDEN SPIDER
(ARGIOPE TRIFASCIATA)

The banded garden spider is a large spider with an egg-shaped body and bright markings. The spider's color varies. Some are reddish brown with white bands. Others are black with white and yellow bands. The spider's legs also have bands in colors similar to its body. Silver hairs cover the spider's neck area. The banded garden spider builds an orb-shaped web in gardens between plants. It sits and waits in the center of its web with its body upside down until prey become stuck in the web.

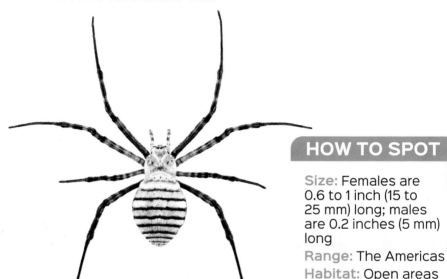

HOW TO SPOT

Size: Females are 0.6 to 1 inch (15 to 25 mm) long; males are 0.2 inches (5 mm) long

Range: The Americas

Habitat: Open areas with tall grasses, plants, and shrubs

Diet: Insects

SPINNERETS

A spinneret is a spider's silk-producing organ. Spinnerets are shaped like tubes or cones. Liquid silk emerges from the spinneret's tip. When the liquid silk hits the air, it forms a filament. The spider draws the silk filament into a thread. Then the spider uses the silk thread to create a web or cocoon covering.

BARN SPIDER *(ARANEUS CAVATICUS)*

The barn spider creates intricate wheel-shaped webs to catch prey. This spider ranges from light brown to dark brown in color. Its abdomen is often reddish brown and covered with tiny hairs that are red and brown. The spider's long legs are thicker at the base and become thin and pointy at the ends. The legs have striped bands of red, brown, and white. Barn spiders capture their prey in sticky webs. Every day at dusk, the spider builds a new web. In the morning it consumes the web and is ready to build again that night.

HOW TO SPOT

Size: Males are 0.2 to 0.4 inches (6 to 10 mm) long; females are 0.5 to 0.6 inches (12 to 16 mm) long

Range: North America

Habitat: Barns, caves, mine openings, and cliff overhangs

Diet: Insects such as mosquitoes, flies, beetles, and moths

BOLD JUMPING SPIDER
(PHIDIPPUS AUDAX)

The bold jumping spider is black with spots and stripes on its abdomen and legs. In young spiders the spots are orange, but they turn white in older spiders. The spider's mouthparts are bright metallic-blue or green. This spider has eight eyes and very good eyesight. It uses its good eyesight to hunt its prey. Like other jumping spiders, the bold jumping spider does not build webs to catch prey. Instead, it actively hunts and stalks its prey during the day. First it watches the prey. Then it sneaks up on the prey and jumps on it.

FUN FACT

When a bold jumping spider leaps, it releases a line of webbing. If the jump fails, the line catches the spider as it falls.

HOW TO SPOT

Size: Males are 0.3 to 0.5 inches (8 to 13 mm) long; females are 0.4 to 0.6 inches (10 to 15 mm) long

Range: Southern Canada and the United States east of the Rocky Mountains

Habitat: Grasslands, prairies, and open woodlands

Diet: Insects

BROWN RECLUSE SPIDER
(LOXOSCELES RECLUSA)

The brown recluse spider has a yellow-brown neck with a brown patch shaped like a violin. Its abdomen is covered with short hairs that look like soft fur. The rest of the spider's body is a darker, reddish brown. This spider has six eyes arranged in three pairs. It also has long, thin legs covered in small hairs. The bite of a brown recluse spider releases a small amount of highly toxic venom. Wounds can be slow to heal. Some bites lead to infections or cause the affected tissue to die.

HOW TO SPOT

Size: Males are 0.3 inches (8 mm) long; females are 0.4 inches (9 mm) long

Range: Midwestern and southern United States

Habitat: Outdoors under rocks and debris; may be found in homes and outbuildings

Diet: Small insects

CAROLINA WOLF SPIDER
(HOGNA CAROLINENSIS)

The Carolina wolf spider is the largest wolf spider species in North America. It is dark brown in color with gray hairs on its neck area. Its underside is black, while its brown abdomen has a dark stripe down the middle. This wolf spider is active during the summer. It is a skilled hunter that seeks out its prey. Though sometimes seen during the day, the giant wolf spider is mainly nocturnal. Its dark coloring helps camouflage it on the ground. The female spins a large egg sac and attaches it to her spinneret. Then she drags the egg sac until her spiderlings hatch.

FUN FACT

After the spiderlings hatch, they climb onto the back of the female Carolina wolf spider. She carries them until they are ready to live on their own.

HOW TO SPOT

Size: Males are 0.8 inches (20 mm) long; females are 0.9 to 1.4 inches (23 to 36 mm) long
Range: United States
Habitat: Various habitats
Diet: Insects

COBWEB SPIDER
(ENOPLOGNATHA OVATA)

The small cobweb spider varies in color and pattern. Its abdomen can be white, cream, or green in color. The spider may also have dark spots on the side of the abdomen, a broad red stripe, or two red stripes in a V pattern. Its legs are translucent. The cobweb spider is a predator. It preys on insects that are much bigger than itself. The female lays eggs in a white sac that gradually becomes blue-gray. The spider hides the egg sac in a rolled-up leaf tied with silk. The female guards the egg sac until the eggs hatch.

HOW TO SPOT

Size: 0.2 inches (5 mm) long
Range: Europe and North America
Habitat: Shrubs, grasslands, and gardens
Diet: Small insects

COMMON HOUSE SPIDER
(ACHAEARANEA TEPIDARIORUM)

Common house spiders are among the most widespread spiders in North America. This spider is often found in houses, barns, storage sheds, fences, and other structures. It ranges in color from yellowish tan to black and has patches of faded color on its back. Its yellow legs have lightly ringed segments, while its abdomen ranges from dull white to brown. The common house spider spins uneven webs that can be spotted in wall and window corners.

HOW TO SPOT

Size: Males are 0.2 inches (4 mm) long; females are 0.2 to 0.3 inches (5 to 8 mm) long
Range: Southern Canada and the United States
Habitat: Dwellings and other structures
Diet: Insects

FUN FACT
A house spider's web is made of many crisscrossing strands of sticky silk.

DESERT TARANTULA
(APHONOPELMA CHALCODES)

The desert tarantula can be found in the deserts and woodlands of the southwestern United States. The spider is mostly black with a brownish-gray neck and a patch of rust-colored stinging hairs on its abdomen. The stinging hairs ward off potential predators. Females are larger and heavier than males and are also lighter in color. The spider is nocturnal and solitary. It often hides in its burrow or under rocks during the day. At night it emerges to search for food. The tarantula bites prey with its fangs and injects it with venom.

HOW TO SPOT

Size: Up to 2.8 inches (71 mm) long

Range: Southwestern United States

Habitat: Desert soil

Diet: Lizards, crickets, beetles, grasshoppers, cicadas, and caterpillars

LONG-BODIED CELLAR SPIDER *(PHOLCUS PHALANGIOIDES)*

The long-bodied cellar spider has a pale, yellow-brown body with a large, gray patch in the center of its cephalothorax. This small spider has a narrow abdomen and very long, thin legs. It spins an irregular web in dark cellars, garages, and other structures. Then it hangs upside down in the web where it waits to capture prey such as insects and other spiders.

FUN FACT

The long-bodied cellar spider is commonly known as the daddy longlegs spider, but it should not be confused with another order of arachnids called harvestmen, which are also nicknamed daddy longlegs.

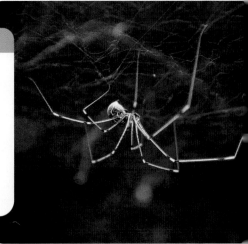

HOW TO SPOT

Size: 0.2 to 0.4 inches (5 to 10 mm) long

Range: Worldwide

Habitat: Under stones and ledges and in low-light locations such as cellars and caves

Diet: Insects and other spiders

RABID WOLF SPIDER
(LYCOSA RABIDA)

The rabid wolf spider is brownish yellow in color with dark stripes. As a nocturnal spider, it actively hunts insect prey at night. The female spins a silk cocoon around her eggs. She attaches the cocoon to her spinnerets and carries it with her. After they hatch, the spiderlings ride on the female's back until they are ready to move on their own.

HOW TO SPOT

Size: Males are 0.5 inches (13 mm) long; females are 0.6 to 0.8 inches (15 to 20 mm) long

Range: Eastern and midwestern United States

Habitat: Woods, meadows, in litter, and on low foliage

Diet: Small insects

FUN FACT

Although they are called rabid wolf spiders, these arachnids do not carry the rabies virus. They get their name from their erratic movements.

SOUTHERN BLACK WIDOW SPIDER *(LATRODECTUS MACTANS)*

The southern black widow spider is a species of venomous spider found in North America. The southern black widow is shiny and black. The female has a red hourglass marking on the underside of her abdomen and red spots on her back. The male has red and white stripes on the sides of his elongated abdomen. The spider has curved bristles on its hind legs that form a comb foot that is used to throw silk over prey. The female black widow's venom is extremely toxic to people. Male black widows do not bite.

HOW TO SPOT

Size: Males are 0.1 inches (3 mm) long; females are 0.4 inches (10 mm) long

Range: Southeastern United States

Habitat: Among fallen branches and under objects such as furniture, trash, and more

Diet: Insects

FUN FACT

After mating, the female black widow sometimes eats the male spider. This is the reason for the word *widow* in the spider's name.

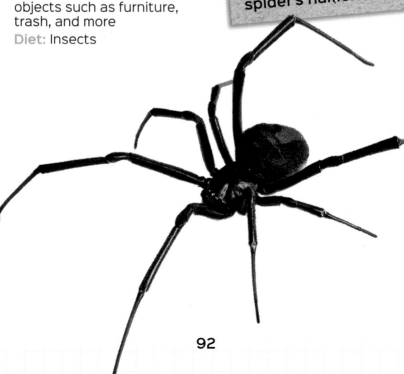

SPITTING SPIDER
(SCYTODES THORACICA)

The spitting spider has a pale, yellow body with black markings that resemble a musical instrument known as a lyre. The spider's long legs have black bands and taper away from the body. Adults are active during the summer inside dwellings. At night they hunt. When it finds prey, the spider spits a sticky substance at it. It covers the prey in numerous overlapping bands of the goo. The material paralyzes the prey. Once the sticky substance dries, the spider bites the prey and injects venom to liquefy its insides. The spider eats its prey by sucking its liquefied tissues.

HOW TO SPOT

Size: Males are 0.1 to 0.2 inches (3 to 4 mm) long; females are 0.2 inches (5 mm) long

Range: Southeastern Canada, the eastern United States, and parts of Europe

Habitat: Temperate forests, dark corners, cellars, cupboards, and closets

Diet: Insects

SYDNEY FUNNEL-WEB SPIDER
(ATRAX ROBUSTUS)

The Sydney funnel-web spider is a venomous spider found in Australia. It has venom sacs and large fangs. The spider is a glossy, blue-black color with fine hairs that cover its abdomen. This spider's legs are shiny. It remains solitary except when mating. The spider builds white silk webs at ground level. It weaves the entrance into a funnel. When an insect lands on the web, the spider quickly approaches the prey and bites it. Then the spider takes the prey into the funnel to feed.

HOW TO SPOT

Size: Males are 1 inch (25 mm) long; females are 1.4 inches (36 mm) long

Range: Australia

Habitat: Gullies, moist soil, and compost heaps

Diet: Beetles, cockroaches, insect larvae, native land snails, millipedes, frogs, and other small vertebrates

FUN FACT
Sydney funnel-web spiders are very fast runners and will bite humans if disturbed. Without immediate treatment, the spider's bite can be fatal.

ZEBRA SPIDER *(SALTICUS SCENICUS)*

Zebra spiders are named for the black and white stripes on their abdomens. Males have large, black fangs that point forward. The zebra spider is a jumping spider. It catches its prey by leaping on it. The spider can leap up to 4 inches (10 cm). When the spider spots large prey, it approaches from behind. The zebra spider jumps on the prey, bites to immobilize it, and then eats it.

HOW TO SPOT

Size: 0.2 to 0.3 inches (4 to 7 mm) long

Range: Europe and the United States

Habitat: Dry, sunny locations; often seen on walls, on fences, and in gardens

Diet: Insects such as flies and mosquitoes

BROWN HARVESTMAN
(PHALANGIUM OPILIO)

The brown harvestman is one of the most widespread species of harvestmen in the world. It has a short, sphere-shaped body and long, thin legs. The upper part of the body is covered with a light-gray or brown pattern, while the lower part is generally light cream in color. Its chelicerae, or jaws, are large and pincer-like. Adults are active in the late spring through early fall. In agricultural fields, they prey on several crop pests.

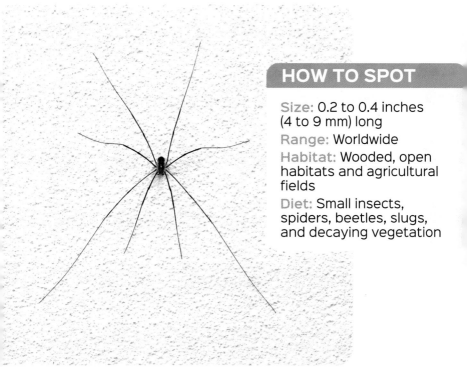

HOW TO SPOT

Size: 0.2 to 0.4 inches (4 to 9 mm) long
Range: Worldwide
Habitat: Wooded, open habitats and agricultural fields
Diet: Small insects, spiders, beetles, slugs, and decaying vegetation

HARVESTMEN

Although they may look similar, a harvestman is not a spider. Harvestmen have two eyes, while spiders can have up to eight eyes. Unlike spiders, harvestmen do not have silk glands and do not spin webs. Harvestmen also do not have fangs or venom as spiders do.

96

EASTERN HARVESTMAN
(LEIOBUNUM VITTATUM)

The eastern harvestman is also known as the striped harvestman because of the large, blackish stripe down the middle of its back and sides. It is yellow to greenish brown in color with long legs that are either pale or dark. The eastern harvestman is active during the late spring through early fall. It is often found resting on leaves, tree trunks, or the walls of buildings in cool, shady areas. To keep warm on cool fall nights, eastern harvestmen will huddle together in tree holes and other sheltered areas.

HOW TO SPOT

Size: 0.2 to 0.3 inches (6 to 8 mm) long
Range: North America
Habitat: Forests, woodlands, parks, and backyards
Diet: Small insects, fungi, and plant fluids

FUN FACT
Harvestmen use the sensitive tips of their legs as sense organs.

97

AMERICAN DOG TICK
(DERMACENTOR VARIABILIS)

The American dog tick is a species that is known for carrying diseases such as Rocky Mountain spotted fever and rabbit fever. As its name suggests, the tick is typically found on dogs. It will sometimes feed on larger animals such as cattle, horses, and humans. The tick moves from host to host to feed on blood. The adult tick is typically brown to reddish brown in color with a round, oval body and eight legs. It also has distinctive gray and silver markings that form diamonds and other geometric designs on its upper back.

HOW TO SPOT

Size: 0.2 to 0.6 inches (5 to 15 mm) long
Range: United States and parts of Canada
Habitat: Forests, wooded areas, and grasslands
Diet: Blood of animals including dogs, rabbits, humans, and raccoons

CLOVER MITE *(BRYOBIA PRAETIOSA)*

The clover mite is a widespread plant-feeding mite. Adults are reddish brown to dark, greenish brown in color. They have eight legs, but their front two legs are twice the size of the other legs. Because the large front legs extend forward near the mite's head, they are sometimes mistaken for antennae. The mite's body is oval-shaped with feather-like plates on its abdomen. Large populations of clover mites can cause damage to lawns, flowers, and other plants. Although they are primarily plant feeders, they can sometimes enter buildings. They do not attack humans.

HOW TO SPOT

Size: 0.03 inches (0.8 mm) long
Range: Worldwide
Habitat: Lawns and other areas with host plants
Diet: A wide range of plants including lawn grasses, ornamental flowers, clovers, dandelions, and more

FUN FACT
When crushed, the clover mite leaves a red stain from its body fluids, which is sometimes mistaken for blood.

DEER TICK *(IXODES SCAPULARIS)*

The deer tick, also known as the black-legged tick, is the main carrier of the human illness called Lyme disease. The tick is generally dark brown to black in color. Females are orange or red behind the scutum, the hard shield behind the tick's head. The adult deer tick has no significant markings and does not have eyes. The tick feeds on the blood of mammals, particularly the white-tailed deer. When it feeds on human hosts, it can spread Lyme disease.

FUN FACT
Deer ticks generally need to feed for about 24 to 48 hours to transmit diseases such as Lyme disease.

HOW TO SPOT

Size: 0.1 inch (3 mm) long
Range: Eastern United States
Habitat: Forests and fields where host animals are common
Diet: Blood of animals such as mice, birds, and deer

AN INFREQUENT FEEDER

Most ticks can survive for 200 days without feeding. In fact, the deer tick only needs to feed three times during its entire life cycle. It needs to feed once during the larval stage, once in the nymph stage, and once as an adult tick.

HARVEST MITE
(NEOTROMBICULA AUTUMNALIS)

The harvest mite is a parasite. Its larvae infest domestic mammals, humans, and some birds. The female lays her eggs in damp soil. After they hatch, the larvae climb grass blades and wait for a host. When one comes near, the larvae attach to the host and feed on its tissue. After several days of feeding, they fall off and develop into nymphs and then, later, adult mites. The larvae are red or orange in color. They have three pairs of long legs covered by claws and bristly hairs. Adult mites are reddish in color and have pentagon-shaped back plates.

HOW TO SPOT

Size: 0.01 inches (0.3 mm) long

Range: Western Europe to southwestern Asia

Habitat: Varied

Diet: Larvae eat the liquefied tissue of hosts; adults eat plant fluids, other insects, and insect eggs

LONE STAR TICK
(AMBLYOMMA AMERICANUM)

The lone star tick is primarily brown in color. It has eight legs and long mouthparts. The name *lone star* refers to a pale white spot near the center of the female's back shield. The male has white streaks or spots around the edges of its body. At all three life stages of the tick (larvae, nymph, and adult), it will feed on humans and other animals. Although the lone star tick does not transmit Lyme disease, it does transmit other diseases. These include Rocky Mountain spotted fever, tularemia (rabbit fever), and ehrlichiosis.

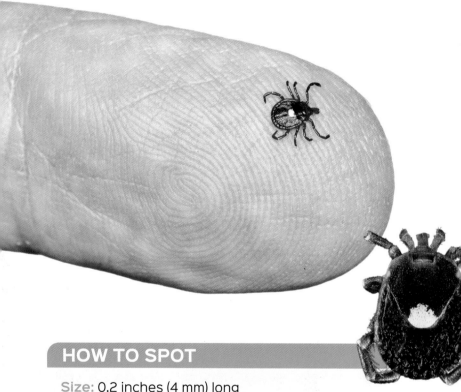

HOW TO SPOT

Size: 0.2 inches (4 mm) long

Range: Eastern, southeastern, and midwestern United States

Habitat: Woodlands where white-tailed deer live

Diet: Blood of mammals and birds

TWO-SPOTTED SPIDER MITE
(TETRANYCHUS URTICAE)

The tiny two-spotted spider mite is a plant-feeding mite that is generally considered a pest. The oval-shaped mite is typically yellowish and almost translucent in color. It has eight legs and a distinct dark spot on each side of its body. As winter approaches, some mites turn reddish orange. Active in the spring through fall, the spider mite can invade areas where plants are abundant, such as greenhouses, gardens, and nurseries. The mite feeds on the plant and removes sap from leaf tissues, which causes the leaves to appear speckled. If severely infested with spider mites, the plant may die.

HOW TO SPOT

Size: Less than 0.01 to 0.03 inches (0.3 to 0.8 mm) long
Range: North America and Europe
Habitat: Gardens, orchards, and greenhouses
Diet: Foliage and fruit

FUN FACT
The dark spots on the two-spotted spider mite's body are food particles that can be seen through the body wall.

ARIZONA BARK SCORPION
(CENTRUROIDES EXILICAUDA)

Arizona bark scorpions are yellowish, medium-size scorpions. They have long, thin pincers and tails. A bark scorpion has a dark stripe down its back. It is one of the most venomous scorpions in the United States and can give a very painful sting. The bark scorpion typically rests during the day under stones, litter, or loose bark. At night it emerges to hunt for food on the ground, tree trunks, and walls. It grabs prey with its claws and quickly kills the prey with a venomous sting.

HOW TO SPOT

Size: Up to 3 inches (7.6 cm) long
Range: Southwestern United States
Habitat: Temperate and dry areas, often under rocks, logs, tree bark, and other objects
Diet: Soft-bodied insects, worms, and other invertebrates

SCORPION VENOM

All scorpions are venomous. A pair of glands produce the scorpion's venom. When the scorpion stings its victim, muscles around the venom glands squeeze. The squeezing forces venom through the stinger and into the wound. The venom causes stinging and burning in the prey. It also contains neurotoxins that affect different parts of the prey's body.

EMPEROR SCORPION
(PANDINUS IMPERATOR)

The emperor scorpion is one of the largest scorpions in the world. Its body is shiny black with two large pincers in front. It has four walking legs and a long tail that ends in a stinger. Its venom is generally mild. To kill prey, the emperor scorpion typically uses its enormous claws to tear its prey apart. Despite its fearsome appearance, the emperor scorpion is often timid. When threatened, it will flee before fighting. However, if cornered, this scorpion will become aggressive. Emperor scorpions are social and live in colonies of up to 15 scorpions. The scorpion rests during the day and emerges at night.

HOW TO SPOT

Size: 7.9 inches (20 cm) long
Range: West Africa
Habitat: Hot and humid forests
Diet: Insects and sometimes small vertebrates

FUN FACT

Because their eyesight is poor, emperor scorpions have sensory structures called pectines behind their legs that help them sense their surroundings.

GIANT DESERT HAIRY SCORPION *(HADRURUS ARIZONENSIS)*

The giant desert hairy scorpion is the largest scorpion in North America. It has a tan to olive-green color with a darker back and yellowish claws, legs, and tail. The scorpion's tail is covered with stiff, brown hairs, explaining the word *hairy* in its name. The scorpion is a solitary predator that is active on warm nights. When hunting, it hides and grabs prey with its front claws and stings the victim with its tail. During the day, the scorpion hides under rocks, in caves, or in burrows. Although not aggressive, the giant desert hairy scorpion will attack when provoked. Its sting is painful but not life-threatening to humans.

HOW TO SPOT

Size: 5.5 inches (14 cm) long

Range: Southwestern United States

Habitat: Deserts

Diet: Insects, lizards, small mammals, and other scorpions

STRIPED BARK SCORPION
(CENTRUROIDES VITTATUS)

The striped bark scorpion is yellowish to tan in color and has two broad, black stripes on its abdomen. It has a dark triangle on top of its head. Like most scorpions, the striped bark scorpion has a flattened, elongated body. It has four pairs of walking legs and a pair of pincers in the front of its body. Its long, curling tail ends in a stinger. The scorpion uses its pincers to capture and hold its prey. Then it stings and kills the prey with its venom-filled tail.

HOW TO SPOT

Size: 1 to 1.5 inches (2.5 to 3.8 cm) long

Range: Southern central United States and northern Mexico

Habitat: Varied, from woodlands to deserts

Diet: Soft-bodied prey such as spiders, cockroaches, ants, crickets, beetles, and butterflies

FUN FACT
Striped bark scorpions are born live rather than in eggs, usually in litters that average about 31 scorpions.

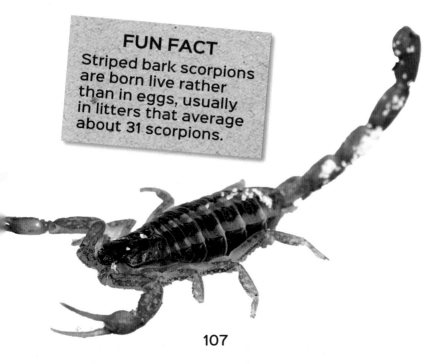

GLOSSARY

abdomen
One of three main body parts of an insect. It is the third segment of the insect's body, after the thorax.

aphid
A small, soft-bodied insect that sucks the juices of plants.

blowout
A valley created by wind in an area with sand or light soil.

cephalothorax
The front part of an arachnid's body.

colony
A group of one species whose members live and interact together.

hibernate
To spend the winter in a dormant state.

larva
The active, juvenile form of an insect.

mandibles
Jaws or jawbones.

mouthpart
A structure near the mouth of an insect that is used to gather or eat food.

nocturnal
Active at night.

pollinator
An insect or animal that moves pollen from one flower to another flower.

predator
An animal that preys on another animal.

prey
An animal that is hunted or killed by another animal for food.

proboscis
In insects, a tube-shaped mouthpart used for feeding.

pronotum
A plate-like structure found on the thorax of some insect species.

secrete
To give off a substance.

thorax
One of three main body parts of an insect. It is the second segment of the insect's body, behind the head and in front of the abdomen.

translucent
Allowing light to pass through.

TO LEARN MORE

FURTHER READINGS

Daniels, Jaret C. *Insects & Bugs for Kids: An Introduction to Entomology*. Adventure Publications, 2021.

Honovich, Nancy. *1,000 Facts about Insects*. National Geographic, 2018.

Romero, Libby. *Insects*. National Geographic, 2017.

ONLINE RESOURCES

To learn more about insects and arachnids, please visit **abdobooklinks.com** or scan this QR code. These links are routinely monitored and updated to provide the most current information available.

PHOTO CREDITS

Cover Photos: Cathy Keifer/iStockphoto, front (moth); iStockphoto, front (green moth), front (Hercules beetle), front (scorpion); Anneliese Gruenwald-Maerkl/iStockphoto, front (ladybug); Tracy Wesolek/iStockphoto, front (tarantula); Shutterstock Images, front (butterfly), front (tick), back (water bug); Andrew Banham/Shutterstock Images, front (long-horned beetle); Cristina Romero Palma/Shutterstock Images, front (fly); Meister Photos/Shutterstock Images, front (harvestman); Alexsander Ovsyannikov/Shutterstock Images, front (spider); Ayhan Turan Menekay/Shutterstock Images, front (hornet); Danut Vieru/Shutterstock Images, back (mosquito); Eric Isselee/Shutterstock Images, back (praying mantis); Tom Biegalski/Shutterstock Images, back (dragonfly)

Interior Photos: Kasira Suda/Shutterstock Images, 1 (beetle), 23; Tig Tillinghast/Shutterstock Images, 1 (hornet), 34 (top); Michael Siluk/Shutterstock Images, 1 (cricket), 77; Shutterstock Images, 1 (tarantula), 5 (fruit fly), 5 (bombardier beetle), 5 (wasp), 11 (top), 13, 15 (top), 16 (top), 20 (bottom), 24, 28, 29 (top), 29 (bottom), 31 (top), 32 (top), 48, 56, 57 (bottom), 58 (top), 58 (bottom), 61, 63 (bottom), 67 (top), 67 (bottom), 69, 71, 72 (top), 76 (bottom), 82, 84, 87 (bottom), 89 (top), 90 (right), 92, 95 (top), 96, 97 (top), 98 (bottom), 100, 101 (top), 102 (right), 105 (top), 107, 112 (top left), 112 (center), 112 (top right); Tobias Hauke/Shutterstock Images, 1 (scorpion), 93 (top), 104; Clint H./Shutterstock Images, 4 (scorpion);

Steve Collender/Shutterstock Images, 4 (spider); Sean McVey/Shutterstock Images, 4 (beetle); Gerald A. DeBoer/Shutterstock Images, 5 (milkweed bug); Petlin Dmitry/Shutterstock Images, 5 (cricket); Keith V./Shutterstock Images, 5 (bee); Super Prin/Shutterstock Images, 5 (butterfly); Sari Oneal/Shutterstock Images, 6 (top), 64 (top), 81 (top), 85 (bottom), 91; Jay Ondreicka/Shutterstock Images, 6 (bottom), 64 (bottom); Cosmin Manci/Shutterstock Images, 7, 65; Arno van Dulmen/Shutterstock Images, 8 (top), 8 (bottom left); Ant Cooper/Shutterstock Images, 8 (bottom right); Keith Hider/Shutterstock Images, 9; Ksenia Lada/Shutterstock Images, 10; iStockphoto, 11 (bottom), 38 (bottom), 44 (top), 50 (top), 85 (top), 103 (bottom); A. S. Floro/Shutterstock Images, 12 (top); Laurie K./iStockphoto, 12 (bottom); Steve Bower/Shutterstock Images, 14, 27 (top); David Birkenfeld/iStockphoto, 15 (bottom); Bildagentur Zoonar GmbH/Shutterstock Images, 16 (bottom); Mario Saccomano/Shutterstock Images, 17; Vinicius R. Souza/Shutterstock Images, 18 (top); Rudmer Zwerver/Shutterstock Images, 18 (bottom); Snelson Stock/Shutterstock Images, 19; Paul Kulinich/Shutterstock Images, 20 (top); Paul Sparks/Shutterstock Images, 21, 78 (bottom); Alf Ribeiro/Shutterstock Images, 22; D. L. Kugler/Shutterstock Images, 25 (top); Daniel Knop/Shutterstock Images, 25 (bottom); Tomasz Klejdysz/Shutterstock Images, 26, 70 (top), 70 (bottom);

ABDOBOOKS.COM

Published by Abdo Publishing, a division of ABDO, PO Box 398166, Minneapolis, Minnesota 55439. Copyright © 2022 by Abdo Consulting Group, Inc. International copyrights reserved in all countries. No part of this book may be reproduced in any form without written permission from the publisher. Abdo Reference™ is a trademark and logo of Abdo Publishing.

Printed in the United States of America, North Mankato, Minnesota.
102021
012022

Editor: Arnold Ringstad
Series Designer: Colleen McLaren
Content Consultant: Dr. Douglas Golick, Associate Professor, Department of Entomology, University of Nebraska-Lincoln

Library of Congress Control Number: 2021941708
Publisher's Cataloging-in-Publication Data
Names: Mooney, Carla, author.
Title: Insects and arachnids / by Carla Mooney
Description: Minneapolis, Minnesota : Abdo Publishing, 2022 |
   Series: Field guides for kids | Includes online resources and index.
Identifiers: ISBN 9781532196973 (lib. bdg.) | ISBN 9781098218782
   (ebook)
Subjects: LCSH: Insects--Juvenile literature. | Arachnids--Juvenile
   literature. | Insects--Behavior--Juvenile literature. | Bug watching--
   Juvenile literature. | Spiders--Juvenile literature | Field guides--
   Juvenile literature
Classification: DDC 595.7--dc23

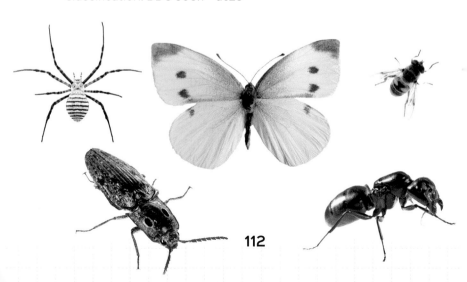